DUDE,
Got Another
JOKE?

Bob Phillips

HARVEST HOUSE PUBLISHERS
Eugene, OR 97402

Cover by Terry Dugan Design, Bloomington, Minnesota

DUDE, GOT ANOTHER JOKE?
Copyright © 2002 by Bob Phillips
Published by Harvest House Publishers
Eugene, Oregon 97402

ISBN-13: 978-0-7369-0455-1
ISBN-10: 0-7369-0455-7

Printed in the United States of America

08 09 10 11 / BC-VS / 14 13 12 11 10 9

Table of Contents

Radical Humor

If you woke up in the night, what would you do
    for a light?
Take a feather from the pillow; that's light enough.

I won't say my house is a mess, but have you
    ever seen a fly land in a cloud of dust?

It's tough to go through an identity crisis when
    you're apathetic. You don't know who you
    are, and you couldn't care less about finding
    the answer.

Football is getting rough. You have to wear
shoulder pads, a face mask, and a helmet . . .
and that's just to sit in the stands.

☆ ☆ ☆

I was a five-letter man my first year in college
and the letters were F-L-U-N-K.

☆ ☆ ☆

Crime is really bad in my old neighborhood. On
Christmas, Santa Claus comes down the
chimney wearing a red suit and a matching
ski mask.

☆ ☆ ☆

Editor to writer: Your book is a first-grade
novel. Unfortunately, most of our readers
have gone beyond the first grade.

☆ ☆ ☆

A man spent a week in the mountains. He left
on Friday and came back on the same
Friday. How did he do it?
His donkey was named Friday.

☆ ☆ ☆

Did you hear about the woman who cooked so many TV dinners that she thought she was in show business?

They say that marriage makes a man dizzy, and it's true. As soon as I got a wife, I lost my balance at the bank.

I was on an airline that was so cheap, when they rolled those little steps away, the plane fell over on its side.

A man came home without his key and found all the doors and windows locked. How did he get in?
He raced around the house until he was "all in."

On our team, we got very few hits. If anybody reached first base, he had to stop and ask for directions.

During a Ping-Pong game, one of the contestants accidentally swallowed the ball. The ambulance came and sped him to the hospital, where he was quickly rushed into the operating room.

When he recovered after the operation, he noticed a dozen scars all over his body, some on his chest, some on his stomach. "Why did you cut me in so many places?" he asked the doctor.

"That's the way the ball bounces," answered the surgeon.

☆ ☆ ☆

A song heard by a hive: "Bee it ever so humble, there's no place like comb."

☆ ☆ ☆

One friend of mine was so stupid he had to take the IQ test twice to get it up to a whole number.

☆ ☆ ☆

A father was trying to break up his daughter's habit of making too many telephone calls. In an effort to slow her down he made a small sign for the telephone, which read:
Is this call really necessary?

The next day he found this sign in its place:
How can I tell until after I have made it?

☆ ☆ ☆

One day two fathers and two sons went fishing.
Each caught a fish. But only three fish were
caught. Why is that?
*Because there were only three fishermen—a boy, his
father, and his grandfather.*

Agatha and Abegayle

Agatha: Which bull led 3,000 elephants over the Alps and conquered Italy?
Abegayle: Search me.
Agatha: Hanni-bull.

☆ ☆ ☆

Agatha: Which candy can't get anywhere on time?
Abegayle: I'm in the dark.
Agatha: Choco-late!

☆ ☆ ☆

Agatha: Which dog eats with its tail?
Abegayle: I don't have the foggiest.
Agatha: All dogs keep their tail on when eating.

☆ ☆ ☆

Agatha: Which food is essential to good music?
Abegayle: I'm blank.
Agatha: The beet!

☆ ☆ ☆

Agatha: Which foods are especially good for
    young people?
Abegayle: That's a mystery.
Agatha: The pro-teens!

☆ ☆ ☆

Agatha: Which Native American Indian tribe
    produced the most lawyers?
Abegayle: I don't know.
Agatha: The Sioux.

☆ ☆ ☆

Agatha: Which vegetable is strong and green?
Abegayle: I pass.
Agatha: A muscle sprout.

☆ ☆ ☆

Agatha: Which famous detective writer was
    white and lacy?
Abegayle: Beats me.
Agatha: Sir Arthur Conan Doily.

☆ ☆ ☆

Agatha: Which western hero was created in a
    science lab?
Abegayle: My mind is a blank.
Agatha: The Clone Ranger.

☆ ☆ ☆

Agatha: Which part of a highway always freezes
    first?
Abegayle: Who knows?
Agatha: The cold shoulder.

☆ ☆ ☆

Agatha: Which cartoon character spends most of
    his time in a basement?
Abegayle: I give up.
Agatha: Popeye the Cellar Man.

☆ ☆ ☆

Agatha: Which fairy story is about a princess
    and seven short wimpy guys?
Abegayle: You tell me.
Agatha: Snow White and the Seven Dorks.

☆ ☆ ☆

Agatha: Which bird is always out of breath?
Abegayle: I have no clue.
Agatha: A puffin.

Open the Door!

Knock, knock.
Who's there?
Nettie.
Nettie who?
You're Nettie as a fruit cake!

Knock, knock.
Who's there?
Cash.
Cash who?
I always knew you were some kind of nut!

Knock, knock.
Who's there?
Dishes.

Dishes who?
Dishes the way I talk now that I've got false
    teeth.

Knock, knock.
Who's there?
Flossie.
Flossie who?
Flossie your teeth every day.

Knock, knock.
Who's there?
Earl.
Earl who?
Earl I want for Christmas is my two front teeth.

Knock, knock.
Who's there?
Freddy.
Freddy who?
Freddy or not here I come!

Knock, knock.
Who's there?
Luke.
Luke who?
Luke out the window and see.

Knock, knock.
Who's there?
Anna.
Anna who?
Anna partridge in a pear tree!

Knock, knock.
Who's there?
Doc.
Doc who?
Doc the halls with boughs of holly!

Knock, knock.
Who's there?
Police.
Police who?
Police open the door. I'm tired of knocking.

☆ ☆ ☆

Knock, knock.
Who's there?
Ben.
Ben who?
Ben over and get your birthday spanking!

Knock, knock.
Who's there?
Zippy.
Zippy who?
Zippy-dee-doo-dah. Zip-a-dee-day.

Knock, knock.
Who's there?
Stopwatch.
Stopwatch who?
Stopwatch you're doing and open this door!

Knock, knock.
Who's there?
Al B.
Al B. who?
Al B. back.

Knock, knock.
Who's there?
Shelby.
Shelby who?
Shelby comin' round the mountain when she
    comes . . .

Knock, knock.
Who's there?
Tubby.
Tubby who?
Tubby or not to be.

Knock, knock.
Who's there?
Ivan.
Ivan who?
Ivan to come in. It's cold out here.

Barnaby and Bailey

Barnaby: Where do cows stay on vacation?
Bailey: Search me.
Barnaby: In moo-tels.

☆ ☆ ☆

Barnaby: Where do giant Eskimos live?
Bailey: I'm in the dark.
Barnaby: In big-loos.

☆ ☆ ☆

Barnaby: Where do detectives sleep?
Bailey: I don't have the foggiest.
Barnaby: Under cover.

☆ ☆ ☆

Barnaby: Where does a skunk sit in church?
Bailey: I'm blank.
Barnaby: In a pew.

Barnaby: Where does a computer whiz keep his
accounts?
Bailey: That's a mystery.
Barnaby: In a data bank.

Barnaby: Where's the best place to drive your
car if you're on a strict diet?
Bailey: I have no idea.
Barnaby: In the fast lane.

☆ ☆ ☆

Barnaby: Where do you find the nerdiest place
in outer space?
Bailey: I don't know.
Barnaby: On the dork side of the moon.

☆ ☆ ☆

Barnaby: Where does Santa Claus keep his red
suit?
Bailey: I pass.
Barnaby: In his Santa Clauset.

☆ ☆ ☆

Barnaby: Where do you buy presents for a cat?
Bailey: Beats me.
Barnaby: In a cat-alogue!

☆ ☆ ☆

Barnaby: Where's the best place to keep these
    little ears of corn?
Bailey: My mind is a blank.
Barnaby: Put them in the corn crib.

☆ ☆ ☆

Barnaby: Where do teenage pigs like to hang
    out?
Bailey: Who knows?
Barnaby: At slopping malls.

☆ ☆ ☆

Barnaby: Where is the best place in the house to
    keep sled dogs?
Bailey: I give up.
Barnaby: In a mush room.

☆ ☆ ☆

Barnaby: Where do you find a tortoise with no
    legs?
Bailey: You tell me.
Barnaby: Where you left it.

☆ ☆ ☆

Barnaby: Where can you always get satisfaction?
Bailey: I have no clue.
Barnaby: From the satis-FACTORY.

☆ ☆ ☆

Barnaby: Where do hamsters come from?
Bailey: I can't guess.
Barnaby: Hamsterdam.

Laugh Out Loud

Amy: How's your new job as a night watchman?
Jerry: I'm really good at it. The slightest noise
    wakes me up.

☆ ☆ ☆

Ricky: I'd like to buy some goose feathers.
Nova: Can you afford the down payment?

☆ ☆ ☆

Employer: Your résumé says you've worked
    about 45 years, but you say you're only 38
    years old! How do you explain that?
Employee: Overtime!

☆ ☆ ☆

They say exercise kills germs, but how do you
get them to exercise?

What do fish sing to each other?
Salmon-chanted Evening.

"I love to eat hot dogs," admitted the boy
frankly.

If crocodile skins make a good pair of shoes,
what do banana skins make?
Good slippers.

Dad: Honey, I can't find my carpentry tools.
Mom: Oh, don't be such a saw loser.

Genevieve: My mother sews, my father weaves,
and my sister crochets.
Gertrude: Sounds like you have a close-knit
family.

They're a perfect match. He's a detective who never solved a case . . . and she's totally clueless.

☆ ☆ ☆

Marcus: So, you're calling me stupid, eh? You'll be sorry!

Jessica: I've always been sorry that you're stupid!

☆ ☆ ☆

Boy: Isn't the principal a dummy?

Girl: Say, do you know who I am?

Boy: No.

Girl: I'm the principal's daughter.

Boy: And do you know who I am?

Girl: No.

Boy: Thank goodness!

☆ ☆ ☆

Latest Computer Best-Sellers
   A Tale of Two CDs
   Gone with the Windows
   War and PC
   Moby Disk

6

Cecil and Cedrick

Cecil: Who had eight guns and terrorized the ocean?
Cedrick: Search me.
Cecil: Billy the Squid.

☆ ☆ ☆

Cecil: Who would I blame if California fell into the Pacific Ocean?
Cedrick: I'm in the dark.
Cecil: It would be San Andreas Fault.

☆ ☆ ☆

Cecil: Who controls congested rabbit highways?
Cedrick: I don't have the foggiest.
Cecil: Hare Traffic Controller.

☆ ☆ ☆

Cecil: Who has large antlers, a high voice and
   wears white gloves?
Cedrick: I'm blank.
Cecil: Mickey Moose.

☆ ☆ ☆

Cecil: Who steals from the rich, gives to the
   poor, and carries a picnic basket?
Cedrick: That's a mystery.
Cecil: Little Red Robin Hood.

☆ ☆ ☆

Cecil: Who delivers Easter treats to all the fish in
   the sea?
Cedrick: I have no idea.
Cecil: The Oyster Bunny!

☆ ☆ ☆

Cecil: Who do bucks and does write to for
   advice?
Cedrick: I don't know.
Cecil: Dear Abby.

☆ ☆ ☆

Cecil: Who are the patron saints of vacations?
Cedrick: I pass.
Cecil: St. Thomas, St. Croix, and San Juan.

Cecil: Who makes suits and eats spinach?
Cedrick: Beats me.
Cecil: Popeye the Tailorman.

Cecil: Who's married to Antarctica?
Cedrick: My mind is a blank.
Cecil: Uncle Arctica.

How Now

How can you make a slow horse fast?
Tie him up.

☆ ☆ ☆

How did the rocket lose its job?
It got fired.

☆ ☆ ☆

How do you make gold stew?
Add 14 carrots.

☆ ☆ ☆

How do you spell cat backward?
C-A-T B-A-C-K-W-A-R-D!

How does the weirdo feel about winter?
It leaves him cold!

How many letters are there in the alphabet?
Eleven . . . T-H-E-A-L-P-H-A-B-E-T.

How does a pilot cook his meals?
In a flying pan.

How did the Three Bears keep Goldilocks from
reentering their house?
They put a Goldi-lock on the door!

How can you keep a fish from smelling?
Stick a Band-Aid across his nose.

How do computers know what to eat?
They read the menu!

How can you buy eggs and be sure they have no
   chickens in them?
Buy duck eggs.

How do you keep food on an empty stomach?
Bolt it down.

How do you make a turtle fast?
Don't feed him.

☆ ☆ ☆

How can you tell a spring chicken?
By the bounce in its step.

The Answer Man

Why does lightning shock people?
Because it doesn't know how to conduct itself.

☆ ☆ ☆

Why is it hard to remember the last tooth you
  had pulled?
Because it went right out of your head.

☆ ☆ ☆

Why don't cannibals eat clowns?
Because they taste funny.

☆ ☆ ☆

Why was the little shoe sad?
His father was a sneaker and his mother was a loafer.

Why did the crow sit on the telephone pole?
He wanted to make a long-distance caw.

Why is a river so rich?
It has two banks all its own.

Why do you call your dog "Fried Egg"?
Because he rolls over easy.

Why would a spider make a good ballplayer?
Because he is good at catching flies.

Why do golfers bring an extra pair of pants with
them when they play golf?
In case they get a hole in one.

☆ ☆ ☆

Why did the boy keep his bicycle in his bedroom?
He was tired of walking in his sleep.

Why did the man bring a bag of feathers to the store?
He wanted to make a down payment.

Why did the mouse run away from home?
Because he found out that his father was a rat.

Why does a dog dress warmer in summer than in winter?
Because in the winter he wears a fur coat, while in summer he wears a coat and pants.

Why did the farmer put corn in his shoes?
To feed his pigeon toes.

Why do firemen wear red suspenders?
To hold up their pants.

What's a good way to keep your house warm?
Put a coat of paint on it.

Why did the exterminator examine his computer?
He heard there was a bug in the system.

Why do farmers from Iowa build their pigsties
between their houses and their barns?
For their pigs.

☆ ☆ ☆

Why did the little hummingbird have to stay
after school?
He didn't do his humwork.

Daphne and Dagmar

Daphne: Who delivers Christmas presents to
  private eyes?
Dagmar: Search me.
Daphne: Santa Clues.

☆ ☆ ☆

Daphne: Who is Santa Claus's wife?
Dagmar: I'm in the dark.
Daphne: Mary Christmas.

☆ ☆ ☆

Daphne: Who conquered half the world, laying
  eggs along the way?
Dagmar: I don't have the foggiest.
Daphne: Attila the Hen.

☆ ☆ ☆

Daphne: Who are the hamburgers' favorite
    people?
Dagmar: I'm blank.
Daphne: Vegetarians!

Daphne: Who can you always rely on in Burger
    Land during an emergency?
Dagmar: That's a mystery.
Daphne: Hamburger helpers!

Daphne: Who tell the best chicken jokes?
Dagmar: I have no idea.
Daphne: Comedi-hens.

Daphne: Knock, knock.
Dagmar: Who's there?
Daphne: José.
Dagmar: José who?
Daphne: José, can you see?

Daphne: Who lost the battle of Waterloo and
    then exploded?
Dagmar: I don't know.
Daphne: Napoleon Blownapart.

Crazy Thoughts

Customer: I'd like a triple-chocolate ice-cream sundae with lots of nuts on top of the whipped cream.
Waiter: How about a cherry on top?
Customer: Golly, no! I'm on a diet.

☆ ☆ ☆

Little boy: Daddy, do you think clams are happy?
Father: Have you ever heard one complain?

☆ ☆ ☆

Jamie: Herbie hides under the sofa and reports every time you're hugged?
Kelly: Yes, he's a regular little press agent.

☆ ☆ ☆

Steve: I'd go to the ends of the earth for you.
Wendy: Yeah, but would you stay there?

Seth: Which baseball team do you like best, the
    Red Sox or the Nylons?
Kyler: The Red Sox.
Seth: But the Nylons get more runs.

Abby: I started life without a penny in my
    pocket.
Hannah: So what? I started life without a pocket.

Mother: Sit down and tell me what your grades
    are in school.
Son: I can't. I just told Pop.

Nit: The surgeon removed a healthy appendix
    with a blunt scalpel.
Wit: What a pointless operation!

Prison Warden: I've been in charge of this prison for ten years. Let's have a celebration. What kind of party do you suggest?
Prisoner: An open house!

☆ ☆ ☆

Zack: I'm exhausted! I was up until midnight doing homework!
Mack: What time did you start?
Zack: Eleven forty-five.

☆ ☆ ☆

Tyler: Did anyone laugh when you fell on the ice?
Travis: No, but the ice made a few cracks.

☆ ☆ ☆

Joe: Are you crazy if you talk to yourself?
Moe: Only if you listen to yourself.

☆ ☆ ☆

Clayton: Where in the world are you going with that candy bag?
Conrad: I've got a 14-carat diamond ring in it, and I'm going to propose to my girl.
Clayton: Do you think she'll accept you?
Conrad: Sure—it's in the bag.

☆ ☆ ☆

Reporter: Why did you go to the North Pole?
Adventurer: Because I wanted to feel on top of
the world.

☆ ☆ ☆

Horace: Did you know that when there's light-
ning, cows hide in trees?
Harry: I never see them.
Horace: See how good they hide?

☆ ☆ ☆

She: Did you get hurt when you were on the
football team?
He: No. It was while the team was on me.

☆ ☆ ☆

Gabriel: My father can hold up an auto with one
hand.
Flora: He must be a very strong man!
Gabriel: Not particularly—he's a policeman!

☆ ☆ ☆

Jonas: I've changed my mind.
Joshua: Well, it can't be any worse than your old
one.

☆ ☆ ☆

Corey: When I went fishing I saw a fish that weighed 20 pounds out of the water.
Carter: How do you know it weighed 20 pounds?
Corey: It had scales on its back.

☆ ☆ ☆

Karl: Did they take an X ray of your sister Sue's jaw at the hospital?
Kyle: They tried to, but the only thing they could get was a motion picture.

☆ ☆ ☆

Becki: Why don't you go home!
Byron: Gee, why?
Becki: So you can brush up on your ignorance!

11

Edgar and Egor

Edgar: Why do hippos paint themselves green?
Egor: Search me.
Edgar: So they can hide in a bowl of spinach.

Edgar: Why do bees have sticky hair?
Egor: I'm in the dark.
Edgar: Because of their honey combs.

Edgar: Why did the runaway elephant wear
    striped pj's?
Egor: I don't have the foggiest.
Edgar: He didn't want to be spotted.

Edgar: Why did the chewing gum cross the road?
Egor: I'm blank.
Edgar: Because it was stuck to the chicken's foot.

☆ ☆ ☆

Edgar: Why do elephants paint their trunks red
and their ears green?
Egor: That's a mystery.
Edgar: So they can hide in rhubarb patches.

☆ ☆ ☆

Edgar: Why did the two volcanoes refuse to talk
to each other?
Egor: I have no idea.
Edgar: They had a lava's quarrel.

☆ ☆ ☆

Edgar: Why did the banana go to the doctor?
Egor: I don't know.
Edgar: Because it wasn't peeling very well.

☆ ☆ ☆

Edgar: Why did the two boa constrictors get
married?
Egor: I pass.
Edgar: They had a crush on each other.

☆ ☆ ☆

44

Edgar: Why did the man keep tripping over lob-
sters?
Egor: Beats me.
Edgar: Because he was accident prawn.

Edgar: Why did the audience throw eggs at the
actor?
Egor: My mind is a blank.
Edgar: Because ham and eggs go well together!

Edgar: Why did the sick skunk stay in bed for a
week?
Egor: Who knows?
Edgar: Doctor's odors.

Edgar: Why did Sue break up with that poet?
Egor: I give up.
Edgar: She just couldn't stanza him anymore.

Edgar: Why did the frog cross the road?
Egor: You tell me.
Edgar: Because it was the chicken's day off.

Edgar: Why is history like a fruitcake?
Egor: I have no clue.
Edgar: Because it's full of dates.

Did You Hear?

Did you hear the one about the boxer? It'll knock you out!

Did you hear the one about the jungle? It's wild!

Did you hear the one about the rocket? It's out of sight.

Did you hear about the train engine that went crazy? It was a loco-motive!

Did you ever hear the story about the two holes
in the ground? Well, well.

Did you hear about the newlyweds who were so
skinny that on their wedding day the guests
didn't throw rice, they threw vitamins?

Did you hear about the worm that joined the
army? He's in the apple corps.

Did you hear the one about the salt mine? It's
pretty deep!

Did you hear the one about the soap cleaner? It's
real clean.

Did you hear the one about the toothache? It's a
pain!

Did you hear the one about the canyon? It's
grand!

Did you hear the joke about the knife? It's a
cut-up.

Did you hear the joke about the bed? It hasn't
been made up yet.

Did you hear the joke about the lunch meat? It's
a lot of baloney.

Did you hear about the dumb crook? He
thought the easiest way to get some fast
dough was to rob bakeries.

Did you hear the one about the sewing machine?
It'll leave you in stitches!

Did you hear the one about the terrible twin boys? It's two bad!

Did you hear about the patient with a split personality? He was so stuck up he wouldn't even speak to himself.

Did you hear about the compulsive golfer? He drove himself insane.

School Daze

Teacher: I wish you would stop whistling while you are studying.
Student: I'm not studying, just whistling.

Teacher: Give me a sentence using the word "politics."
Student: A parrot named Polly swallowed a watch, and now Polly ticks.

Teacher: What was your mother's name before she was married?
Student: I think it must have been Hilton. That's the name on our towels.

Two girls were talking quietly at the back of the
class.
"That boy over there really annoys me," said
Jenny.
"But he's not even looking at you," answered
Janey.
"I know, that's what's annoying me," said Jenny.

Teacher: What's the best way to pass this geom-
etry test?
Boy: Knowing all the angles?

Jimmy: Did Noah really build an ark?
Teacher: When I get to heaven I'll ask him.
Jimmy: But what if he didn't go to heaven?
Teacher: Then you can ask him.

Dannie: Did the music teacher really say you
had a heavenly voice?
Nicki: Not exactly. She said it was like nothing
on earth.

Teacher: Kendall, how can one person make so many stupid mistakes on one day?

Kendall: I get up early.

☆ ☆ ☆

Teacher: Class, tomorrow you'll be taking an aptitude test.

Student: No fair! You didn't teach aptitude this semester!

☆ ☆ ☆

Professor: Today I'm going to lecture on the heart, kidneys, liver, and lungs.

Premed student: Oh great! Another organ recital!

☆ ☆ ☆

Principal: Now, Sylvia, did you really call your teacher a meany?

Sylvia: Yes, I did.

Principal: And is it true you called her a wicked old witch?

Sylvia: Yes, it is.

Principal: And did you call her a tomato-nosed beanbag?

Sylvia: No, but I'll remember that one for next time!

Driving instructor: Do you know what a green light means?

Teen student: It means go.

Driving instructor: Do you know what a red light means?

Teen student: It means stop.

Driving instructor: Do you know what a yellow light means?

Teen student: Yes. It means go fast so you don't have to stop.

☆ ☆ ☆

Teacher: Kent, what are the four main food groups?

Kent: Canned, Frozen, Instant, and Lite.

☆ ☆ ☆

Teacher: Gordon, do you use bad words?

Gordon: No, teacher.

Teacher: Do you disobey your parents?

Gordon: No, teacher.

Teacher: Come now, what do you do that's naughty?

Gordon: I tell lies.

☆ ☆ ☆

Kindergarten teacher: Can you tie your shoes well?

Jimmy: Knot always.

☆ ☆ ☆

Teacher: All right, Joslyn, let's hear you count to ten.
Joslyn: One, two, three, four, five, six, seven, eight, nine, ten.
Teacher: That's fine, Joslyn. Can you go a little higher?
Joslyn: Jack, Queen, King!

☆ ☆ ☆

Teacher: Lindsey, you forgot the dot over the i.
Lindsey: I didn't forget. It's still in the pencil.

Who's There?

Knock, knock.
Who's there?
Oliver.
Oliver who?
Oliver long way away.

☆ ☆ ☆

Knock, knock.
Who's there?
Kenya.
Kenya who?
Kenya guess?

☆ ☆ ☆

Knock, knock.
Who's there?
York.
York who?
York, york, york. This is funny.

Knock, knock.
Who's there?
Tic tac.
Tic tac who?
Tic tac paddy whack, give the dog a bone.

Knock, knock.
Who's there?
Francis.
Francis who?
Francis next to Germany.

Knock, knock.
Who's there?
Larry.
Larry who?
Larry up and let me in.

Knock, knock.
Who's there?
Ears.
Ears who?
Ears looking at you kid.

Knock, knock.
Who's there?
Havana.
Havana who?
Havana great time here!

Knock, knock.
Who's there?
Cheese.
Cheese who?
Cheese a jolly good fellow.

Knock, knock.
Who's there?
Jamaica.
Jamaica who?
Jamaica mistake?

58

Knock, knock.
Who's there?
Frank.
Frank who?
Frank you very much.

Knock, knock.
Who's there?
Adair.
Adair who?
Adair you to open this door.

Knock, knock.
Who's there?
Omar.
Omar who?
Omar goodness, what are you doing in there?

Knock, knock.
Who's there?
Little old lady.
Little old lady who?
I didn't know you could yodel.

Knock, knock.
Who's there?
Red.
Red who?
Red any good knock knock joke books lately?

☆ ☆ ☆

Knock, knock.
Who's there?
Franz.
Franz who?
Franz, Romans, countrymen, lend me your ears.

Gallager and Garfield

Gallager: What do you call two spiders who just got married?
Garfield: Search me.
Gallager: Newlywebs.

Gallager: What's the difference between a gossip and a mirror?
Garfield: I'm in the dark.
Gallager: One speaks without reflecting and one reflects without speaking.

Gallager: What is a frog's favorite drink?
Garfield: I don't have the foggiest.
Gallager: Croaka-cola.

Gallager: What do you give a seasick elephant?
Garfield: I'm blank.
Gallager: Plenty of room.

☆ ☆ ☆

Gallager: What is the difference between a fisherman and a lazy schoolboy?
Garfield: I have no idea.
Gallager: One baits his hook, the other hates his book.

☆ ☆ ☆

Gallager: What is everyone in the world doing now?
Garfield: I don't know.
Gallager: Growing older.

☆ ☆ ☆

Gallager: What do you call two bikes that look exactly alike?
Garfield: I pass.
Gallager: Identical Schwinns.

☆ ☆ ☆

Gallager: What goes "krab, krab?"
Garfield: Beats me.
Gallager: A dog barking backward.

☆ ☆ ☆

Gallager: What's a tired tent called?
Garfield: My mind is a blank.
Gallager: A sleepy teepee.

☆ ☆ ☆

Gallager: What four letters of the alphabet
would frighten a thief?
Garfield: Who knows?
Gallager: O I C U.

☆ ☆ ☆

Gallager: What is a duck's favorite TV program?
Garfield: I give up.
Gallager: The feather forecast.

☆ ☆ ☆

Gallager: What kind of snake loves dessert?
Garfield: You tell me.
Gallager: A pie-thon, of course.

☆ ☆ ☆

Gallager: What is the difference between a crazy
hare and a counterfeit coin?
Garfield: I have no clue.
Gallager: One is a mad bunny, the other is a bad
money.

☆ ☆ ☆

Gallager: What do you get if you cross a karate
    expert with a tree?
Garfield: I can't guess.
Gallager: Spruce Lee.

☆ ☆ ☆

Gallager: What crime did the thief commit in the
    bakery?
Garfield: Search me.
Gallager: A pie-jacking!

☆ ☆ ☆

Gallager: What would you get if you crossed a
    fuzzy yellow bear with a virus?
Garfield: I'm in the dark.
Gallager: Winnie the Flu!

☆ ☆ ☆

Gallager: What did the beaver say to the tree?
Garfield: I don't have the foggiest.
Gallager: It's been nice gnawing you.

☆ ☆ ☆

Gallager: What do you call a deer who's a wimp?
Garfield: I'm blank.
Gallager: A namby-pamby Bambi!

Frida and Fergus

Frida: Why did the whale cross the ocean?
Fergus: Search me.
Frida: To get to the other tide.

Frida: Why is this bread full of holes?
Fergus: I'm in the dark.
Frida: It's whole-wheat bread.

Frida: Why did the turkey cross the road?
Fergus: I don't have the foggiest.
Frida: The chicken retired and moved to Florida.

64

Frida: Why do rats have long tails?
Fergus: I'm blank.
Frida: They can't remember short stories.

☆ ☆ ☆

Frida: Why did the bacterium cross the microscope?
Fergus: That's a mystery.
Frida: To get to the other slide.

☆ ☆ ☆

Frida: Why hasn't this rocket been shot into space yet?
Fergus: I have no idea.
Frida: The crew is on its launch break.

☆ ☆ ☆

Frida: Why did the cookie visit the doctor?
Fergus: I don't know.
Frida: He felt crummy.

☆ ☆ ☆

Frida: Why did the blonde stare at the can of frozen orange juice for two hours?
Fergus: I pass.
Frida: Because the can said "concentrate."

Frida: Why don't fish go near computers?
Fergus: Beats me.
Frida: They're afraid of getting caught in the
Internet.

☆ ☆ ☆

Frida: Why are you bringing cheese into the
computer room?
Fergus: My mind is a blank.
Frida: You told me I was going to work with a
mouse today.

☆ ☆ ☆

Frida: Why does it take so long to build a blonde
snowman?
Fergus: Who knows?
Frida: You have to hollow out the head.

☆ ☆ ☆

Frida: Why did the blonde quit her job as a rest-
room attendant?
Fergus: I give up.
Frida: She couldn't figure out how to refill the
hand dryer.

☆ ☆ ☆

Frida: Why is my mail so soggy?
Fergus: You tell me.
Frida: Postage dew.

Tell Me Why

Why was the birthday cake as hard as a rock?
Because it was marble cake!

Why is an empty coin purse always the same?
Because there's no change in it.

Why did the pig farmer rush off in such a hurry?
He had to do some last-minute Christmas slopping.

Why did you put that lamp in your bed?
I'm a light sleeper!

Why are skeletons usually so calm?
Nothing gets under their skin.

Why do dogs bury bones in the ground?
Because you can't bury them in the trees.

Why did the otter cross the road?
To get to the otter side.

Why did the mole go to the bank?
To burrow money.

Why was the cat so small?
It only drank condensed milk.

Why didn't the elephant cross the road?
Because he didn't want to be mistaken for a chicken.

Why did the chicken cross the road at the fair-
ground?
To get to the other ride.

☆ ☆ ☆

Why do dogs run in circles?
It's hard to run in squares.

☆ ☆ ☆

Why do elephants have such big trunks?
They have to travel all the way from Africa.

How About It?

How do you get an elephant upstairs?
In an ele-vator.

☆ ☆ ☆

How does a hungry man eat a hot dog?
With relish!

☆ ☆ ☆

How does a leopard change its spots?
*When it gets tired of one spot it just moves to
 another.*

☆ ☆ ☆

How did the rabbits survive the car crash?
Dual Hare Bags.

☆ ☆ ☆

How many environmentalists does it take to
change a light bulb?
*If the light bulb is out, that's the way nature intended
it!*

☆ ☆ ☆

How many paranoids does it take to change a
light bulb?
Who wants to know?

☆ ☆ ☆

How many Russian leaders does it take to
change a light bulb?
*Nobody knows. Russian leaders don't last as long as
light bulbs.*

☆ ☆ ☆

How many lawyers does it take to change a light
bulb?
How many can you afford?

☆ ☆ ☆

How many software people does it take to screw
in a light bulb?
None. That's a hardware problem.

How did George Washington speak to his army?
In general terms!

How do you repair a broken tuba?
With a tuba glue.

How can you tell the difference between our
    legal system and a skating rink?
One is justice, the other's just ice.

How should you send a letter to the Easter
    Bunny?
By hare mail!

☆ ☆ ☆

How can you tell that you're getting old?
*You go to an antique auction and three people bid on
    you!*

Silly Dillies

Joe: I had a terrible nightmare last night.
Moe: How bad was it?
Joe: Real bad. I dreamt I was a muffler. I woke
    up exhausted.

☆ ☆ ☆

Mom: How was school today, Janie?
Janie: It was good. We learned how to make
    babies!
Mom: Is that so? And . . . um . . . how do you
    make babies?
Janie: It's easy. Just take away the "y" and put
    on "i," "e," and "s"!

☆ ☆ ☆

Show me a coal miner who wears a flashlight on
    his helmet, and I'll show you a guy whose
    work makes him lightheaded.

☆ ☆ ☆

Peggy: I can't get a baby-sitter who actually pays
attention to the kids!
Echo: Oh, I solved that problem: I just put the
baby on top of the TV!

☆ ☆ ☆

Christy: I think I'll fix lunch.
Jon-Mark: I didn't know it was broken.

☆ ☆ ☆

Norm: I just spilled root beer all over the stove.
Patsy: Oh great! Foam on the range.

☆ ☆ ☆

Do pigs ever go crazy?
No. But sometimes they go hog wild.

☆ ☆ ☆

A ham raced a hot dog and a hamburger. Who won?
The hot dog—because he was a born wiener.

☆ ☆ ☆

If fish lived on land, which country would they
live in?
Finland.

☆ ☆ ☆

Son: Mom, our dog is a nuisance. He chases
 everyone on a bicycle. What can I do?
Mom: Take his bike away.

☆ ☆ ☆

Judge: The charge is stealing a blanket. How do
 you plead?
Crook: Not quilty.

☆ ☆ ☆

Cowboy: I once saw a bed ten-feet long and ten-
 feet wide.
Foreman: Ah, that's a lot of bunk.

☆ ☆ ☆

Joel: My family says I'll never amount to
 anything!
Debbie: Why, that's not true! With your experi-
 ence, you could be a wonderful "terrible
 example"!

☆ ☆ ☆

Melodie: I just won 30 days of free ice cream.
Mike: Wow! Talk about a month of sundaes.

Hector and Harlow

Hector: What tree can you hold in your hand?
Harlow: Search me.
Hector: A palm.

Hector: What kind of doctor would a duck become?
Harlow: I'm in the dark.
Hector: A quack doctor.

☆ ☆ ☆

Hector: What three letters make a man of a boy?
Harlow: I don't have the foggiest.
Hector: A-G-E.

Hector: What is the difference between a well-dressed man and a tired dog?
Harlow: I'm blank.
Hector: The man wears an entire suit, the dog just pants.

☆ ☆ ☆

Hector: What is the main reason for using a cookie sheet?
Harlow: That's a mystery.
Hector: For cookies to sleep on.

☆ ☆ ☆

Hector: What happens to a man who starts home to dinner and misses his train?
Harlow: I have no idea.
Hector: He catches it when he gets home.

☆ ☆ ☆

Hector: What is the best thing to take when one is run down?
Harlow: I don't know.
Hector: The license number of the car.

Hector: What kind of teeth can you buy for a
    dollar?
Harlow: I pass.
Hector: Buck teeth.

☆ ☆ ☆

Hector: What's worse than finding half a worm
    in your apple?
Harlow: Beats me.
Hector: Finding a frog in your throat.

☆ ☆ ☆

Hector: What do electricians study in school?
Harlow: My mind is a blank.
Hector: Current events!

☆ ☆ ☆

Hector: What letter is most useful to a deaf
    woman?
Harlow: Who knows?
Hector: The letter A, because it makes her hear.

☆ ☆ ☆

Hector: What is the best name for the wife of a
    train conductor in charge of the sleeping
    cars?
Harlow: I give up.
Hector: Bertha.

☆ ☆ ☆

Hector: What dessert is appropriate for a shoe-maker?
Harlow: You tell me.
Hector: Cobbler.

☆ ☆ ☆

Hector: What kind of gum do bees make?
Harlow: I have no clue.
Hector: Bumble gum.

☆ ☆ ☆

Hector: What has a beard and no legs?
Harlow: I can't guess.
Hector: A chin.

☆ ☆ ☆

Hector: What is the difference between a new five-cent piece and an old-fashioned quarter?
Harlow: Search me.
Hector: Twenty cents.

☆ ☆ ☆

Hector: What has 18 legs and catches flies?
Harlow: I'm in the dark.
Hector: A baseball team.

☆ ☆ ☆

Hector: What is the best name for the wife of a
fisherman?
Harlow: I don't have the foggiest.
Hector: Nettie.

Leftovers

Boy: Darling, I could die for your sake.
Girl: You are always saying that, but you never do it.

☆ ☆ ☆

Moe: I'm going to sneeze.
Joe: At who?
Moe: At-choo!

☆ ☆ ☆

Kyle: I told my mirror a joke yesterday.
Nathan: What happened?
Kyle: It cracked up.

☆ ☆ ☆

Suzie: Mummy, why does it rain?
Mother: To make things grow. To give us apples,
    pears, corn, flowers—
Suzie: Then why does it rain on the pavement?

Father: Congratulations! You talked on the
    phone for only 45 minutes instead of the
    usual two hours! What happened?
Daughter: Well, it was the wrong number.

Magician: I can turn a handkerchief into a bou-
    quet of flowers.
Boy: That's nothing. I can go to the corner and
    turn into a drugstore.

Little leaguer: Dad, what does a ballplayer do
    when his eyesight starts going bad?
Dad: He gets a job as an umpire.

Molly: My cat can say his own name.
Marcy: What is your cat's name?
Molly: Meow.

☆ ☆ ☆

Red: My dog knows math.
Fred: Really?
Red: Yes, I ask him what 27 minus 27 is, and he
   says nothing.

☆ ☆ ☆

Billy: I make money with my drums.
Willy: Oh, you play with a band?
Billy: Nope, my pop gives me a dollar a week
   not to play them.

☆ ☆ ☆

Mother: Were you a good little boy at kindergarten today?
Son: Yes, you can't get into much trouble
   standing in the corner all day.

☆ ☆ ☆

Tex: Did you hear about the barn that turned to
   stone?
Rex: No, what happened?
Tex: The wind blew so hard it made the barn
   rock.

Ted: Where does a 680-pound gorilla sleep?
Ned: Where?
Ted: Wherever he wants to!

☆ ☆ ☆

Customer: Are you supposed to tip the waiters around here?
Waiter: Well, yes, sir.
Customer: Then how about tipping me? I've been waiting for two hours.

☆ ☆ ☆

Mack: I left my watch upstairs.
Jack: Don't worry—it will run down.

☆ ☆ ☆

Hotel clerk: Please wipe the mud off your shoes when you come into this establishment.
Clyde: What shoes?

☆ ☆ ☆

Basketball player: We're going to win this game!
Basketball coach: I certainly hoop so.

☆ ☆ ☆

Junior: Dad, I can't find my baseball mitt.
Dad: Look in the car.
Junior: I did, but I couldn't find it.
Dad: Did you try the glove compartment?

Isaac and Isabel

Isaac: What is Santa's favorite Easter candy?
Isabel: Search me.
Isaac: Jollybeans!

☆ ☆ ☆

Isaac: What cowboy hero fought crabgrass
throughout the West?
Isabel: I'm in the dark.
Isaac: The Lawn Ranger!

☆ ☆ ☆

Isaac: What follows a cat wherever he goes?
Isabel: I don't have the foggiest.
Isaac: His tail.

☆ ☆ ☆

Isaac: What dog stands the best chance of winning the heavyweight title?
Isabel: I'm blank.
Isaac: A boxer, of course!

Isaac: What do you get when you cross a computer with an elephant?
Isabel: That's a mystery.
Isaac: A computer with extra memory!

Isaac: What is the best name for the wife of an astronomer?
Isabel: I have no idea.
Isaac: Stella.

Isaac: What is the best name for the wife of a shoemaker?
Isabel: I don't know.
Isaac: Peggy.

Isaac: What is the surest way to keep water from coming into your house?
Isabel: I pass.
Isaac: Don't pay your water bill.

☆ ☆ ☆

Isaac: What asks no questions but receives lots of
answers?
Isabel: Beats me.
Isaac: A telephone.

☆ ☆ ☆

Isaac: What is green and bumpy, and leaps over
buildings in a single bound?
Isabel: My mind is a blank.
Isaac: Super Pickle!

☆ ☆ ☆

Isaac: What's the difference between an elephant
and a flea?
Isabel: Who knows?
Isaac: An elephant can have fleas, but a flea can
never have an elephant.

☆ ☆ ☆

Isaac: When did the pig give his girlfriend a box
of candy?
Isabel: I give up.
Isaac: It was Valenswine's Day!

Isaac: What's black and white, white and black, and green?
Isabel: You tell me.
Isaac: Two skunks fighting over a pickle.

☆ ☆ ☆

Isaac: What would you call a leopard that never takes a bath?
Isabel: I have no clue.
Isaac: The Stink Panther!

☆ ☆ ☆

Isaac: What happens when you feed lemons to a cat?
Isabel: I can't guess.
Isaac: You get a sour puss.

☆ ☆ ☆

Isaac: What is the difference between an old ten-dollar bill and a new one?
Isabel: Search me.
Isaac: Nine dollars.

Jessie and Jeremy

Jessie: What do you get if you cross a thousand years with a thousand chocolate cakes?
Jeremy: Search me.
Jessie: The start of a new millenni-yum-yum!

☆ ☆ ☆

Jessie: What do you call a lion that writes snappy songs?
Jeremy: I'm in the dark.
Jessie: King of the Jingle.

☆ ☆ ☆

Jessie: What's red and blue and makes a mess?
Jeremy: I'm blank.
Jessie: Colored scrambled eggs.

☆ ☆ ☆

Jessie: What did the dog say when he sat on some sandpaper?
Jeremy: That's a mystery.
Jessie: "Ruff."

☆ ☆ ☆

Jessie: What do you call a girl with a frog on her head?
Jeremy: I have no idea.
Jessie: Lily.

☆ ☆ ☆

Jessie: What happened when the cows got out of their field?
Jeremy: I don't know.
Jessie: There was udder chaos.

☆ ☆ ☆

Jessie: What do they serve at birthday parties in heaven?
Jeremy: I pass.
Jessie: Angel food cake, of course!

☆ ☆ ☆

Jessie: What do you call a woman who set fire to the gas bill?

Jeremy: Beats me.
Jessie: Bernadette.

Jessie: What do you call a joke book for
chickens?
Jeremy: My mind is a blank.
Jessie: A yolk book.

Jessie: What's gray, has one ear, and paints?
Jeremy: Who knows?
Jessie: Vincent Van Elephant.

Jessie: What medical advice did the doctor give
Samson?
Jeremy: I give up.
Jessie: Take two pillars and call me in the
morning.

Jessie: What's the scariest dinosaur of them all?
Jeremy: You tell me.
Jessie: A Terrordactyl.

Jessie: What floats, has big guns, and is covered
    with wool?
Jeremy: I have no clue.
Jessie: A battlesheep.

☆ ☆ ☆

Jessie: What is the difference between a tick and
    a lawyer?
Jeremy: I can't guess.
Jessie: A tick falls off you when you die.

Food for Fun

Waitress: Have I kept you waiting long?
Customer: No, but did you know that there are
3,479 rose patterns on your wallpaper?

Customer: Waiter, there's a fly in my chop suey.
Waiter: That's nothing. Wait'll you see what's in
your fortune cookie.

☆ ☆ ☆

Diner: Waiter, what is that fly doing in my
alphabet soup?
Waiter: Learning to read, sir.

☆ ☆ ☆

Customer: There's a fly in the bottom of my tea cup, waiter. What does this mean?
Waiter: How do I know? I'm a waiter, not a fortune-teller.

Customer: Why do you call these metric cookies?
Baker: They're gram crackers.

Diner: Waiter, what's this insect in my soup?
Waiter: How should I know? I'm a waiter, not an entomologist.

Waiter: Why do you keep grunting?
Chef: I'm a snort-order cook.

Customer: Waiter, there's a fly in my soup.
Waiter: It's possible. The cook used to be a tailor.

Diner: Do you have lobster tails?
Waiter: Certainly, sir: Once upon a time, there was a little lobster . . .

☆ ☆ ☆

Waiter: Tonight's special is snails.
Diner: And I see you have them dressed as waiters.

☆ ☆ ☆

Rocko: I know a restaurant where you can eat dirt cheap.
Jocko: But who wants to eat dirt?

☆ ☆ ☆

Diner: Waiter, take back this salad! The dressing has pieces of brick in it!
Waiter: Of course, sir. You asked for the house dressing.

☆ ☆ ☆

Customer: Waitress, there's a fly in my soup!
Waitress: Don't worry, sir. Nothing has ever been known to live very long in our soup.

☆ ☆ ☆

Diner: What are your breakfast specials?
Waitress: Today we're offering hippopotamus eggs and elephant eggs.
Diner: Give me the hippo eggs. I'm tired of elephant yokes.

☆ ☆ ☆

Diner: Waiter, waiter, there's a bird in my soup.
Waiter: That's all right, sir. It's bird's nest soup.

The Answer Man

Why is a pig in the house like a house afire?
Because the sooner it is put out the better.

☆ ☆ ☆

Why is a lie like a wig?
Because it is a false hood.

☆ ☆ ☆

Why did the hockey player color his teeth
   orange?
So they'd be easier to find on the ice.

☆ ☆ ☆

Why did the boy take a ladder to the ball game?
Because the Giants were playing.

Why can't a bicycle stand by itself?
Because it's two tired.

Why did the baker quit making doughnuts?
He was sick of the hole business!

Why was the basketball player holding his nose?
Someone was taking a foul shot.

Why do you always insist on talking about the
weather to your barber?
*You wouldn't have me talk about anything as
exciting as politics to a man who is handling a
razor, would you?*

Why did the man bring a rope to the baseball
game?
To tie up the score.

Why did the boy sleep on the chandelier?
Because he was a light sleeper.

Why does a preacher have an easier time than a
    doctor or a lawyer?
Because it is easier to preach than to practice.

Why is a lawyer like a crow?
Because he likes to have his cause heard.

Why are fishermen and shepherds not to be
    trusted?
Because they live by hook and by crook.

Why does Santa Claus always go down the
    chimney?
Because it soots him.

Why is Joe such a pain in the kitchen?
*He whips the cream, strains the soup, and makes the
    beef stew.*

Why don't astronauts get hungry in space?
Because they just had a launch.

Why is a bride always unlucky on her wedding day?
Because she does not marry the best man.

☆ ☆ ☆

Why should we not believe one word that comes from Holland?
Because Holland is such a low-lying country.

Katie and Kelly

Katie: What do pirates set their table with?
Kelly: Search me.
Katie: Long John Silverware.

☆ ☆ ☆

Katie: What would you get if you crossed a
    comedian with a bicycle?
Kelly: I'm in the dark.
Katie: Someone who is wheel funny.

☆ ☆ ☆

Katie: What do you need when you have three
    lawyers up to their necks in cement?
Kelly: I don't have the foggiest.
Katie: More cement.

☆ ☆ ☆

Katie: What did the rooster say when he walked
into the cow barn?
Kelly: I'm blank.
Katie: Cock-a-doodle-moo!

☆ ☆ ☆

Katie: What did the bull say to the cow?
Kelly: That's a mystery.
Katie: When I fall in love it will be for heifer.

☆ ☆ ☆

Katie: What are high-rise flats for pigs called?
Kelly: I have no idea.
Katie: Styscrapers.

☆ ☆ ☆

Katie: What do you call a dog with a bunch of
daisies on its head?
Kelly: I don't know.
Katie: A collie flower.

☆ ☆ ☆

Katie: What did the paper clip say to the magnet?
Kelly: I pass.
Katie: I find you very attractive.

☆ ☆ ☆

Katie: What kinds of jokes do vegetables like best?
Kelly: Beats me.
Katie: Corny ones!

☆ ☆ ☆

Katie: What should you do if you find a gorilla sitting at your school desk?
Kelly: My mind is a blank.
Katie: Sit somewhere else.

☆ ☆ ☆

Katie: What birds spend all their time on their knees?
Kelly: Who knows?
Katie: Birds of prey.

☆ ☆ ☆

Katie: What kind of fish will help you hear better?
Kelly: I give up.
Katie: A herring aid.

☆ ☆ ☆

Katie: What flies through the jungle singing opera?

Kelly: You tell me.
Katie: The parrots of Penzance.

☆ ☆ ☆

Katie: What happened to that couch potato who
used to sell furniture in this store?
Kelly: I have no clue.
Katie: He probably got sacked.

Odds and Ends

Waitress: Would you like your coffee black?
Customer: What other color do you have?

☆　☆　☆

Bill: I'm not myself today.
Jill: Yeah, I've noticed the improvement.

☆　☆　☆

Daughter: Aw, shucks, ma. Why do I have to
   wash my face again before dinner?
Mother: Because you've got a smudge on it, hon.
Daughter: Why can't I just powder over it like
   you do?

☆　☆　☆

Mary: Do you make up these jokes yourself?
Larry: Yes, out of my head.
Mary: You must be.

☆ ☆ ☆

Randy: I'm nobody's fool.
Florence: Well, maybe someone will adopt you.

☆ ☆ ☆

Edna: Don't you think they make a perfect
couple?
Elsie: Yes, I do. He's a pill, and she's a headache.

☆ ☆ ☆

Orin: Know what I'm going to be when I grad-
uate?
Owen: A senior citizen?

☆ ☆ ☆

Arnold: Did you know that bowling is the
quietest sport?
Burt: No, how can that be?
Arnold: You can hear a pin drop!

☆ ☆ ☆

Overheard (a college gal to friend): Jerry and I are going to have a secret marriage. Jerry doesn't even know about it yet.

☆ ☆ ☆

First sheep: Baa-a-a.
Second sheep: Moo-o-o.
First sheep: Moo-o-o? Why do you say Moo-o-o?
Second sheep: I'm learning a foreign language.

☆ ☆ ☆

First Actress: (behind the scenes): Did you hear the way the public wept during my death scene?
Second Actress: Yes, it must have been because they realized that it was only acting!

☆ ☆ ☆

First explorer: Look! Here's a lion's track!
Second explorer: Great! You find out where he went, and I'll find out where he came from.

☆ ☆ ☆

Justin: Did you know that Daniel Boone's brothers were all famous doctors?
Julius: No.
Justin: Don't tell me you've never heard of the Boone Docs?

☆ ☆ ☆

Bert: Do you think anyone can predict the future with cards?

Curt: My mother can. She takes one look at my report and tells me what will happen when my father comes home.

☆ ☆ ☆

Husband: Where is yesterday's newspaper?

Wife: I wrapped the garbage in it.

Husband: Darn it! I wanted to see it.

Wife: There wasn't much to see—just some orange peels and coffee grounds.

☆ ☆ ☆

Big sister: What did you learn in school today?

Little brother: Algebra.

Big sister: Say something in algebra.

Little brother: Pi r squared.

Big sister: No, no! Pie are round, cornbread are square!

☆ ☆ ☆

Norris: If you had a choice, would you rather be in a collision or an explosion?

Boris: A collision.

Norris: Why?

Boris: Because in a collision, there you are. But in an explosion, where are you?

Clint: Have you been to Cape Kennedy?
Flint: Yes, it's a blast!

Have you ever heard of a baby raised on elephant's milk?
Yes, a baby elephant.

Juliet: Romeo, Romeo, where art thou?
Romeo: Down here in the bushes—the trellis broke!

Christy: See you later, alligator.
Bob: After awhile, Gomer Pyle.

Edgar: A snake bit me.
Eldon: Put something on it.
Edgar. I can't—it slithered away.

Lambert and Laszlo

Lambert: What did Mr. Fog say to Ms. Mist?
Laszlo: Search me.
Lambert: Let's dew lunch sometime.

Lambert: What would you do if a 500-pound
gorilla sat in front of you at the movies?
Laszlo: I'm in the dark.
Lambert: Miss most of the movie.

☆ ☆ ☆

Lambert: What does a baby computer call its
father?
Laszlo: I don't have the foggiest.
Lambert: Data.

☆ ☆ ☆

Lambert: What do you call a baby kangaroo who does nothing but watch television?
Laszlo: I'm blank.
Lambert: A pouch potato.

☆ ☆ ☆

Lambert: What was the outcome of the baseball game played on the Ark?
Laszlo: That's a mystery.
Lambert: A Noah-hitter.

☆ ☆ ☆

Lambert: What do you get if you cross a dog and a frog?
Laszlo: I have no idea.
Lambert: A Croaker Spaniel.

☆ ☆ ☆

Lambert: What did the beaver say to the tree?
Laszlo: I don't know.
Lambert: It sure is good to gnaw you.

☆ ☆ ☆

Lambert: What kind of family spends its time collecting CDs?
Laszlo: I pass.
Lambert: A disk-functional family.

☆ ☆ ☆

Lambert: What do you call a girl who lies in the
middle of a tennis court?
Laszlo: Beats me.
Lambert: Annette.

☆ ☆ ☆

Lambert: What kind of stories do bakers tell
their children?
Laszlo: My mind is a blank.
Lambert: Breadtime stories.

☆ ☆ ☆

Lambert: What do you get if you cross an ele-
phant with a kangaroo?
Laszlo: Who knows.
Lambert: Great big holes all over Australia.

☆ ☆ ☆

Lambert: What do you call a fish with no eyes?
Laszlo: I give up.
Lambert: Fsh.

☆ ☆ ☆

Lambert: What do you get if you cross poison
ivy with a four-leaf clover?

Laszlo: I have no clue.
Lambert: A rash of good luck.

Lambert: What do astronomers do to relax?
Laszlo: I can't guess.
Lambert: They enjoy reading comet books.

Knock, Knock

Knock, knock.
Who's there?
Peas.
Peas who?
Peas to meet you.

Knock, knock.
Who's there?
Sacha.
Sacha who?
Sacha lot of questions in this exam!

Knock, knock.
Who's there?
Candice.
Candice who?
Candice be the last knock-knock joke?

Knock, knock.
Who's there?
Albert.
Albert who?
Albert you'll never guess.

Knock, knock.
Who's there?
Gorilla.
Gorilla who?
Gorilla cheese sandwich for me, will you?

Knock, knock.
Who's there?
Stan.
Stan who?
Stan back, I'm going to break the door down

Knock, knock.
Who's there?
Yukon.
Yukon who?
Yukon open the door—it's safe.

Knock, knock.
Who's there.
I, Toad.
I, Toad who?
I Toad you I was coming over!

Knock, knock.
Who's there?
Avis.
Avis who?
A visitor standing on the porch.

Knock, knock.
Who's there?
Kenya.
Kenya who?
Kenya give me a hand?

Knock, knock.
Who's there?
Luke.
Luke who?
Luke through the keyhole and you'll see.

Knock, knock.
Who's there?
Heaven.
Heaven who?
Heaven seen you for ages!

Knock, knock.
Who's there?
Handsome.
Handsome who?
Handsome candy through the door and I'll tell
    you.

Knock, knock.
Who's there?
Jester.
Jester who?
Jester minute, I'm looking for my key.

Gags Galore

Tailor: Would you like me to rent you a tuxedo, sir?
Customer: That'll suit me fine.

☆ ☆ ☆

Actor: My looks are my fortune.
Agent: Well, you're facing bankruptcy.

☆ ☆ ☆

Charlie: Look at that airplane pilot. Why is he grinning like that?
Farlee: He's trying to accumulate frequent flyer smiles.

☆ ☆ ☆

What goes "Quack-quack!" and fights crime?
Duck Tracy.

Aunt Suzie: Well, Linda, how do you like going
   to school?
Linda: I don't mind going, and I don't mind
   coming home. It's staying there in between
   that I hate.

Roses are red.
Pansies are purple.
Drink too much pop
And you're liable to burple.

My sister thinks I'm too nosy—at least that is
   what she writes in her diary.

Willard: Ouch! A bee stung me on the finger!
Sylvia: Which one?
Willard: How can I tell? All bees look alike!

Fran: My dog can chase a stick for three miles.
Dan: Sounds far-fetched.

☆ ☆ ☆

Show me a king with a sore throat...and I'll
show you a royal pain in the neck!

☆ ☆ ☆

Sign in restaurant: Dinner Special: Turkey $2.35;
Chicken or Beef $2.25; Children $2.00.

☆ ☆ ☆

What kind of humor do you like?

"Sight gags," said the optometrist.
"Slapstick," said the hockey player.
"Dry humor," said the diaper maker.
"Running gags," said the jogger.
"Corny jokes," said the farmer.

☆ ☆ ☆

Bob: It's a real dollars and cents wedding.
Rob: What do you mean?
Bob: He doesn't have a dollar...and she has no
sense.

31

Mabel and Madison

Mabel: What kind of jokes does a chiropodist like?
Madison: Search me.
Mabel: Corny jokes.

☆ ☆ ☆

Mabel: What is soft and cuddly and goes "Oink, oink"?
Madison: I'm in the dark.
Mabel: A teddy boar.

☆ ☆ ☆

Mabel: What did the alphabet say after it fell down?
Madison: I don't have the foggiest.
Mabel: I-M-O-K.

☆ ☆ ☆

Mabel: What's the happiest animal in the wild?
Madison: I'm blank.
Mabel: The happypotamus.

☆ ☆ ☆

Mabel: What's the difference between a monkey
  and a politician?
Madison: That's a mystery.
Mabel: You can hold a sensible conversation
  with a monkey.

☆ ☆ ☆

Mabel: What has feathers and operates an 18-
  wheeler?
Madison: I have no idea.
Mabel: A cluck driver.

☆ ☆ ☆

Mabel: What do you call a very rude bird?
Madison: I don't know.
Mabel: A mockingbird.

☆ ☆ ☆

Mabel: What's yellow, plastic, and holds up
  banks?
Madison: I pass.
Mabel: A robber duckie.

★ ★ ★

Mabel: What do music teachers give you?
Madison: Beats me.
Mabel: Sound advice.

★ ★ ★

Mabel: What's worse than an elephant on water skis?
Madison: My mind is a blank.
Mabel: A porcupine on a rubber life raft.

★ ★ ★

Mabel: What is the hamburger's most familiar song?
Madison: Who knows?
Mabel: Home on the Range!

★ ★ ★

Mabel: What adventure movie features sword-fighting squirrels?
Madison: I give up.
Mabel: The Tree Musketeers.

★ ★ ★

Mabel: What do you call a duck test pilot?
Madison: You tell me.
Mabel: A flyer quacker.

More "Did You Hear?"

Moe: Did you hear there's a new movie about a convict who escapes from prison during a tornado?
Joe: What's it called?
Moe: Con with the Wind.

☆ ☆ ☆

Harry: Did you hear the joke about the lion?
Larry: No.
Harry: When you hear it you will roar.

☆ ☆ ☆

Bill: Did you hear about Lenny the Loafer?
Will: No, what about him?
Bill: He is so lazy that he sticks his nose out the window so that the wind will blow it for him.

✩ ✩ ✩

Jason: Did you see the doctor about your
    memory problem?
Jacob: I certainly did.
Jason: Well, what did he do?
Jacob: He made me pay in advance.

✩ ✩ ✩

Melba: Did you hear the riddle about the front
    door?
Pam: No, but I bet it's a knock-knock joke.

✩ ✩ ✩

Lisa: Did you know that women are smarter
    than men?
Ryan: No, I didn't.
Lisa: See what I mean?

✩ ✩ ✩

Bud: Did you hear about the cowboy who mar-
    ried a cowgirl?
Jan: What kind of marriage is that?
Bud: Western Union.

Stacey: Did you hear about the terrible accident?
A pink cruise ship collided with a purple
cruise ship.
Barry: What happened!
Stacey: All the passengers were marooned!

☆ ☆ ☆

DeeDee: Did you hear about the romance in the
tropical fish tank?
Jeff: No, what happened!
DeeDee: It was a case of guppy love.

☆ ☆ ☆

Alisa: Did you hear about the ten-year-old flag?
Matt: No, what about it?
Alisa: It had a flappy birthday.

☆ ☆ ☆

Christy: Did you hear about the restaurant on
Mars?
Jon-Mark: No.
Christy: The food is great, but there's no atmo-
sphere.

☆ ☆ ☆

Corrie: Did you hear about the tornado who married a twister?

Jeff: No.

Corrie: It was a whirlwind romance.

☆ ☆ ☆

Mr. Horse: Did you hear about the swine who bought a million acres of farmland for development?

Ms. Cow: Wow! What a ground hog!

Nellie and Norma

Nellie: What happened when the lion ate the
comedian?
Norma: Search me.
Nellie: He felt funny.

☆ ☆ ☆

Nellie: What's the best thing to do for a poor
memory?
Norma: I'm in the dark.
Nellie: Just forget about your problem.

☆ ☆ ☆

Nellie: What did the rabbit say when he fell into
a hole filled with water?
Norma: I don't have the foggiest.
Nellie: Oh, well.

✩ ✩ ✩

Nellie: What do you call a nine-foot high stack
of frogs?
Norma: I'm blank.
Nellie: A toadem pole.

✩ ✩ ✩

Nellie: What was Dr. Jekyll's favorite game?
Norma: That's a mystery.
Nellie: Hyde and Seek.

✩ ✩ ✩

Nellie: What do you call a camel with no humps?
Norma: I have no idea.
Nellie: A horse.

✩ ✩ ✩

Nellie: What do you get if you cross a pig and a
red light?
Norma: I don't know.
Nellie: A stop swine.

✩ ✩ ✩

Nellie: What do you call a boy with one foot in
the door?
Norma: I pass.
Nellie: Justin.

☆ ☆ ☆

Nellie: What goes "baaa-baaa-ka-boom?"
Norma: Beats me.
Nellie: A lamb mine.

☆ ☆ ☆

Nellie: What would you do with a sick wasp?
Norma: My mind is a blank.
Nellie: Take it to the waspital.

☆ ☆ ☆

Nellie: What would you get if you crossed a
    sheep and an African monkey?
Norma: Who knows?
Nellie: A baaaaa-boon.

☆ ☆ ☆

Nellie: What do you call a woman who can't
    stop buying romantic fiction?
Norma: I give up.
Nellie: A heroine addict.

☆ ☆ ☆

Nellie: How can you tell a male turkey from a
    female turkey?
Norma: You tell me.

Nellie: The male is the one holding the remote control.

☆ ☆ ☆

Nellie: What would you get if you crossed the Easter Bunny with Chinese food?
Norma: I have no clue.
Nellie: Hop suey!

How Come?

"How's your sick horse?" one rancher asked
   another.
"She's in stable condition."

☆ ☆ ☆

How do you make a bandstand?
Hide all their chairs.

☆ ☆ ☆

How do you fuel a vegetable-powered car?
Fill it up with aspara-gas.

☆ ☆ ☆

How do mountains hear?
With their mountaineers.

How did the beautician break out of prison?
With a lock of hair.

How do you make an artichoke?
Strangle it.

How is cat food sold?
Purr can.

How do you stop your dog from barking in the hall?
Put him in the garden.

How do you help an injured alligator?
Call for Gator Ade.

How many actors does it take to change a light bulb?
Only one. They don't like to share the spotlight.

How do you put a baby astronaut to sleep?
Rocket.

How do you slow down a speeding computer?
Use the disk brakes.

How many morons does it take to screw in a
    light bulb?
*Five. One to hold the bulb in the socket, and four to
    rotate the moron.*

How do you save a drowning lawyer?
Take your foot off his head.

Olaf and Olga

Olaf: What's big and fierce and is worn around
your neck?
Olga: Search me.
Olaf: A Tie-Rannosaurus.

Olaf: What does the girlfriend of Mickey Mouse
drive?
Olga: I'm in the dark.
Olaf: A minnie van.

Olaf: What's the difference between a school-
teacher and a monster?
Olga: I don't have the foggiest.
Olaf: Not a lot!

☆ ☆ ☆

Olaf: What's the difference between getting
    splattered by a water balloon and getting
    smeared by an egg?
Olga: I'm blank.
Olaf: It's the difference between getting soaked
    and getting yolked.

☆ ☆ ☆

Olaf: What do you call a reindeer with one eye
    and no legs?
Olga: That's a mystery.
Olaf: Still no idea. (Still no-eye deer.)

☆ ☆ ☆

Olaf: What's worse than finding a caterpillar in
    your salad?
Olga: I have no idea.
Olaf: Finding half a caterpillar.

☆ ☆ ☆

Olaf: What is always coming but never arrives?
Olga: I don't know.
Olaf: Tomorrow.

☆ ☆ ☆

Olaf: What do you call a man with a seagull on his head?
Olga: I pass.
Olaf: Cliff.

☆ ☆ ☆

Olaf: What's the hottest letter of the alphabet?
Olga: Beats me.
Olaf: B. It makes oil boil.

☆ ☆ ☆

Olaf: What do gnus read in the morning?
Olga: My mind is a blank.
Olaf: The gnus' paper.

☆ ☆ ☆

Olaf: What is a parrot's favorite game?
Olga: Who knows?
Olaf: Hide and speak.

☆ ☆ ☆

Olaf: What do you call a penguin in the desert?
Olga: I give up.
Olaf: Lost.

☆ ☆ ☆

Olaf: What's lemonade?
Olga: You tell me.
Olaf: Helping an old lemon across the road.

☆ ☆ ☆

Olaf: What would you get if you crossed a very dumb person with the English king in 1776?
Olga: I have no clue.
Olaf: King George the Nerd!

Lots of Laughs

Friend: Is that your brother?
Sister: Yes.
Friend: He's very short, isn't he?
Sister: Well, he's only my half brother!

☆ ☆ ☆

Father: Would you like a pocket calculator for
    Christmas, son?
Barney: No thanks, Dad. I know how many
    pockets I've got.

☆ ☆ ☆

Wendy: My pet wolf has a bad habit of hanging
    out with other wolves.
Steve: What's wrong with that?
Wendy: He's up to two packs a day.

☆ ☆ ☆

Passing by a floral shop, a man spied a sign that
said, "Say It with Flowers."
Stepping inside, he said to the clerk, "I'd like a
flower, please."
"Just one flower?" the clerk asked.
"Yes," the man replied. "I'm a man of few
words."

☆ ☆ ☆

Father: You sure cleaned up the garden fast.
Son: I'm a speed weeder.

☆ ☆ ☆

Makena: Do you know why snowmen get cold
feet in bed?
Kyler: Sure. They sleep on sheets of ice.

☆ ☆ ☆

Zach: I guess I didn't get my birthday wish.
Mack: How do you know?
Zach: You're still here!

☆ ☆ ☆

Do turkeys have good table manners?
No. They always gobble up their food.

☆ ☆ ☆

Son: I'm too tired to do my homework tonight.
Mom: A little hard work never killed anyone yet.
Son: Right. But why should I risk being the first?

☆ ☆ ☆

Teacher: Is there any difference between a wild
    horse and a tame horse?
Student: Only a bit.

☆ ☆ ☆

Jill: Is it true your cat had a litter?
Bill: Not really. Turned out she swallowed a ball
    of yarn and gave birth to mittens.

☆ ☆ ☆

Bobby: I don't think my mom knows much
    about children.
Buddy: Why do you say that?
Bobby: Because she always puts me to bed when
    I'm wide awake, and gets me up when I'm
    sleepy!

☆ ☆ ☆

Laurie: A fool can ask more questions than a wise
    man can ever answer. Did you know that?
Brent: Nope.

I'd tell you the joke about the broken pencil . . .
but what's the point?

I was up all night wondering where the sun
went when it set . . . finally, it dawned on me.

☆ ☆ ☆

Lane: Someday I'd like to ride on a submarine.
Tyler: Not me! I wouldn't set foot on any ship
that sinks on purpose!

☆ ☆ ☆

Tourist: A nice man just sold me the city of
Cairo.
Guide: Egypt you!

A policeman stopped a motorist for driving
down a one-way street. "Just where do you
think you're going?" the policeman asked.
"I don't know," answered the confused driver.
"But I must be late. Everyone else is already
coming back."

☆ ☆ ☆

Willy: Watch me make this mud disappear.
Warren: No thanks. I'm not interested in dirty
    tricks.

Paddy and Page

Paddy: What goes "oink-oink," plays classical
    music, and gets a free ride?
Page: Search me.
Paddy: Piggy Bach.

☆ ☆ ☆

Paddy: What has bread on both sides and
    frightens easily?
Page: I'm in the dark.
Paddy: A chicken sandwich.

☆ ☆ ☆

Paddy: What kind of snacks do computers
    munch?
Page: I don't have the foggiest.
Paddy: Microchips.

☆ ☆ ☆

Paddy: What happened to the mouse who was
    sent to Congress?
Page: I'm blank.
Paddy: He was just named Squeaker of the
    House.

☆ ☆ ☆

Paddy: What do you get if you cross a snake
    with a government employee?
Page: That's a mystery.
Paddy: A civil serpent.

☆ ☆ ☆

Paddy: What do you call the study of shopping?
Page: I have no idea.
Paddy: Buy-ology.

☆ ☆ ☆

Paddy: What do you call an elephant with no
    teeth?
Page: I don't know.
Paddy: Gumbo.

☆ ☆ ☆

Paddy: What was the fly doing in the alphabet
    soup?

Page: I pass.
Paddy: Learning to spell.

☆ ☆ ☆

Paddy: What do you call a dinosaur that steps
    on everything in its way?
Page: Beats me.
Paddy: Tyrannosaurus Wrecks.

☆ ☆ ☆

Paddy: What was the name of the hunter who
    tangled with the bear?
Page: My mind is a blank.
Paddy: Claude.

☆ ☆ ☆

Paddy: What do you call a crab that only buys
    ice cream for himself?
Page: Who knows?
Paddy: Shellfish.

☆ ☆ ☆

Paddy: What do you call an arctic cow?
Page: I give up.
Paddy: An eskimoo.

Paddy: What do you call a person who makes up bad jokes as he jogs in a marathon?
Page: You tell me.
Paddy: A cross-country punner.

Paddy: What did the blonde get on her S.A.T. test?
Page: I have no clue.
Paddy: Nail polish.

Laugh Awhile

Hettie: What are you reading?
Betty: A book about electricity.
Hettie: Current events?
Betty: No, just light reading.

☆ ☆ ☆

Girl: Mom, you know you're always worried about me failing math?
Mom: Yes.
Girl: Well, your worries are over.

☆ ☆ ☆

Bradey: Do you write with your right hand or your left hand?
Laney: My right hand.
Bradey: That's funny. I usually use a pencil.

☆ ☆ ☆

Teacher: Do you know who Ivanhoe was?
Student: Er, a Russian gardener?

☆ ☆ ☆

Kristen: Our teacher is like the Mona Lisa.
Tim: You mean she smiles a lot?
Kristen: No, she's so old she should be in a
    museum!

☆ ☆ ☆

Teacher: Can you name four days of the week
    beginning with the letter "T"?
Pupil: Tuesday, Thursday, Today, and Tomorrow!

☆ ☆ ☆

Loralee: Our school must have very clean
    kitchens.
Paul: How can you tell?
Loralee: All the food tastes of soap.

☆ ☆ ☆

Susie: What do you call a teacher floating on a
    raft in the sea?
Mike: I don't know.
Susie: Bob.

☆ ☆ ☆

Teacher: Your homework looks as if it is in your
father's handwriting.
Student: Well, I used his pen, sir.

☆ ☆ ☆

Father: Would you like me to help you with
your homework?
Son: No thanks, I'd rather get it wrong by
myself.

☆ ☆ ☆

Teacher: That's an excellent essay for someone
your age.
Student: How about for someone my mom's age,
teacher?

☆ ☆ ☆

Camille: I was the teacher's pet last year.
Alisa: Why was that?
Camille: She couldn't afford a dog.

☆ ☆ ☆

Teacher: You weren't at school last Friday. I
heard you were out playing football.
Student: That's not true, sir. And I've got the
movie cinema tickets to prove it.

☆ ☆ ☆

Teacher: Name a legendary creature that was half man and half beast.
Pupil: Buffalo Bill.

☆ ☆ ☆

Teacher: What's the difference between ignorance and apathy?
Student: I don't know, and I don't care!

Sonny and Salisbury

Sonny: What weighs three tons, is gray, and flies?
Salisbury: Search me.
Sonny: A hippo on a hang glider.

☆ ☆ ☆

Sonny: What do you call a man with a spade on his head?
Salisbury: I'm in the dark.
Sonny: Doug.

☆ ☆ ☆

Sonny: What ocean animal is the most difficult to get along with?
Salisbury: I don't have the foggiest.
Sonny: The crab.

☆ ☆ ☆

Sonny: What's it called when pigs do their laundry?
Salisbury: I'm blank.
Sonny: Hogwash.

☆ ☆ ☆

Sonny: What do you call a girl with one foot on either side of the river?
Salisbury: That's a mystery.
Sonny: Bridget.

☆ ☆ ☆

Sonny: What's a cowboy dinosaur called?
Salisbury: I don't know.
Sonny: Tyrannosaurus Tex.

☆ ☆ ☆

Sonny: What do you call a man who's a talented painter?
Salisbury: I pass.
Sonny: Art.

☆ ☆ ☆

Sonny: What do you call a group of people who dig for fossils?
Salisbury: Beats me.

Sonny: A skeleton crew.

☆ ☆ ☆

Sonny: What's the biggest problem politicians
     suffer from in Washington?
Salisbury: My mind is a blank.
Sonny: Truth decay.

☆ ☆ ☆

Sonny: What do you call great bodies filled with
     grape juice?
Salisbury: Who knows?
Sonny: The Grape Lakes.

☆ ☆ ☆

Sonny: What do you get if you cross a burglar
     with a concrete mixer?
Salisbury: I give up.
Sonny: A hardened criminal.

☆ ☆ ☆

Sonny: How many cooks does it take to stuff a
     turkey?
Salisbury: You tell me.
Sonny: One, but you really have to squeeze him
     in!

☆ ☆ ☆

Sonny: What would you get if you crossed a
   purple dinosaur with an Irish landmark?
Salisbury: I have no clue.
Sonny: The Barney Stone!

Why Did You Ask?

Why did Jim's grandpa put his hand to his
    mouth when he sneezed?
To catch his teeth.

Why did the baby turkey bolt down his food?
Because he was a little gobbler.

Why did the science teacher take a ruler to bed?
So he could see how long he slept.

Why did you let the air out of the tires on your
    new bike?
So I can reach the pedals!

Why did the dirty chicken cross the road?
For some fowl purpose.

Why did the nurse write on Benny's toes?
He was just adding a footnote.

Why does everybody like to get together at the
local hamburger joint?
It's a perfect meating place!

Why did the elephant cross the road?
To pick up the flattened chicken.

Why did the tomato blush?
Because he saw the salad dressing.

☆ ☆ ☆

Why did they arrest the music teacher?
He got into treble.

Why did the robber have a bath?
So he could get a clean getaway.

Why did the idiot sleep under his car?
So he would wake up oily in the morning.

Why was the little Egyptian girl upset?
Because her daddy was a mummy.

41

Doctor, Doctor

Patient: Doctor! Doctor! I've just swallowed a sheep.
Doctor: How do you feel?
Patient: Very B-A-A-A-A-D.

✫ ✫ ✫

Patient: Doctor, doctor, I keep thinking I'm getting smaller.
Doctor: Well, you'll just have to be a little patient.

✫ ✫ ✫

Patient: Doctor, doctor, I keep thinking I'm a goat.
Doctor: How long have you felt like this?
Patient: Since I was a kid.

☆ ☆ ☆

Patient: Doctor, doctor, I keep thinking I'm a pair of curtains.
Doctor: Oh, pull yourself together.

☆ ☆ ☆

Patient: Doctor! Doctor! I feel like an old sock.
Doctor: Well, I'll be darned.

☆ ☆ ☆

Patient: Doctor! Doctor! I keep seeing frogs before my eyes.
Doctor: Don't worry, it's just a hoptical illusion.

☆ ☆ ☆

Patient: Doctor, doctor, I don't like all these flies buzzing around my head.
Doctor: Pick out the ones you like and I'll swat the rest.

☆ ☆ ☆

Patient: Doctor, doctor, my wife thinks she's a duck.
Doctor: You better bring her in to see me straight away.
Patient: I can't do that—she's already flown south for the winter.

☆ ☆ ☆

Patient: Doctor! Doctor! I feel like a pack of cards.
Doctor: Take a seat and I'll deal with you later.

☆ ☆ ☆

Patient: Doc, I think I'm a rubber band.
Doctor: Isn't that stretching it a bit?

☆ ☆ ☆

Patient: Doctor! Doctor! I can't sleep. What shall I do?
Doctor: Try lying on the edge of the bed. You'll soon drop off.

☆ ☆ ☆

Patient: Doctor! Doctor! People think I'm crazy because I like hamburgers.
Doctor: There's nothing crazy about that. I like hamburgers too.
Patient: Do you? Would you like to come and see my collection?

☆ ☆ ☆

Patient: Doctor, doctor, I've just swallowed the film from my camera.
Doctor: Well, let's hope nothing develops.

☆ ☆ ☆

Doctor: Is there any insanity in your family?
Patient: Yes, my husband thinks he's the boss.

☆ ☆ ☆

Patient: Doctor, doctor, I've got carrots growing
out of my ears!
Doctor: How did that happen?
Patient: I don't know, I planted onions.

☆ ☆ ☆

Patient: Doctor, doctor, I think I'm a garbage bin.
Doctor: Don't talk such rubbish.

Reba and Rene

Reba: What's a pretzel's favorite dance routine?
Rene: Search me.
Reba: The Twist.

☆ ☆ ☆

Reba: What is the egg capital of the world?
Rene: I'm in the dark.
Reba: New Yolk City.

☆ ☆ ☆

Reba: What kind of injury did Humpty Dumpty
   suffer when he fell off the wall?
Rene: I don't have the foggiest.
Reba: Shell shock.

☆ ☆ ☆

Reba: What kind of crazy bird yells "Polly wants a cracker" when he jumps out of an airplane?
Rene: I'm blank.
Reba: A parrot-trooper.

☆ ☆ ☆

Reba: What kind of tea makes you fearless?
Rene: I have no idea.
Reba: Safe-ty.

☆ ☆ ☆

Reba: What do you get if you cross an elephant and a rooster?
Rene: I don't know.
Reba: An animal that never forgets to wake you up in the morning.

☆ ☆ ☆

Reba: What's the very lowest game you can play?
Rene: I pass.
Reba: Baseball.

☆ ☆ ☆

Reba: What do you call a flea that lives in an idiot's ear?
Rene: Beats me.
Reba: A space invader.

☆ ☆ ☆

Reba: What did the hamburger say to the pickle?
Rene: My mind is a blank.
Reba: You're dill-icious!

☆ ☆ ☆

Reba: What kind of cars do cats drive?
Rene: Who knows?
Reba: Catillacs.

☆ ☆ ☆

Reba: What music do bungee jumpers listen to?
Rene: I give up.
Reba: Big Band.

☆ ☆ ☆

Reba: What kind of shoes are made with no
     leather?
Rene: You tell me.
Reba: Horseshoes.

☆ ☆ ☆

Reba: What do Sir Galahad and King Arthur
     watch at 6 o'clock?
Rene: I have no clue.
Reba: The Knightly News.

☆ ☆ ☆

Reba: What kind of vegetable do you find under elephant's feet?
Rene: I can't guess.
Reba: Squash.

Daffy Dictionary

Archaeologist: A scientist whose career lies in ruins.

☆ ☆ ☆

Astronomer: A night watchman.

☆ ☆ ☆

Bowling alley: A place where pin pals meet.

☆ ☆ ☆

Bookworm: A highly educated worm.

☆ ☆ ☆

Computer gossip: Chat rumors.

Cloud bank: A place to save money for a rainy day.

Diet doctor: A man whose patients are wearing thin.

Flypaper: What kites are made of.

Dr. Frankenstein: The first champion bodybuilder.

Grandfather clock: An old timer.

Hangnail: A hook for your jacket.

Illiterate: Write today for free help.

Kneecap: A hat for covering your knee.

Massage therapist: A cramp counselor.

Minister: A man who is the soul support of his
family.

Minnehaha: A very, very small joke.

Naval destroyer: A hula hoop with a nail in it.

Outpatient: Someone who faints in the doctor's
office.

Psychologist: A person who encourages you to
speak freely and then charges you for lis-
tening.

Real estate agent: A person whose job it is to put you in your place.

Retirement fund: Money put aside in case your car gets a flat.

Riverbank: Where tadpoles save their money.

Stopwatch: What a cop yells to a runaway Timex.

Sunbathing: A fry in the ointment.

Sycamore tree: The sickest tree in the forest.

Traffic light: Apparatus that automatically turns red when your car approaches.

Violinist: A musician who does nothing but fiddle around.

Quentin and Quimby

Quentin: What are the worst six years in a
   blonde's life?
Quimby: Search me.
Quentin: Third grade.

☆ ☆ ☆

Quentin: What do you get if you cross an auto-
   mobile with a kangaroo?
Quimby: I don't have the foggiest.
Quentin: A car that jump-starts itself.

☆ ☆ ☆

Quentin: What happens when 50 rabbits hop
   backwards at the same time?
Quimby: I'm blank.
Quentin: You get a receding hare line.

☆ ☆ ☆

Quentin: What musical instrument is found in the bathroom?
Quimby: That's a mystery.
Quentin: A tuba toothpaste.

☆ ☆ ☆

Quentin: What sits at the bottom of the sea and shivers?
Quimby: I have no idea.
Quentin: A nervous wreck.

☆ ☆ ☆

Quentin: What is a pig's favorite ballet?
Quimby: I don't know.
Quentin: Swine Lake.

☆ ☆ ☆

Quentin: What does a clam do on his birthday?
Quimby: I pass.
Quentin: He shellabrates!

☆ ☆ ☆

Quentin: What's the best way to locate missing hares?
Quimby: Beats me.
Quentin: Comb the area.

☆ ☆ ☆

Quentin: What do dieting cannibals eat?
Quimby: My mind is a blank.
Quentin: Thin people.

☆ ☆ ☆

Quentin: What is yellow on the outside, gray in the inside, and has a good memory?
Quimby: I give up.
Quentin: An elephant omelet.

☆ ☆ ☆

Quentin: What do you call a teacher with a tennis racket on her head?
Quimby: You tell me.
Quentin: Annette.

☆ ☆ ☆

Quentin: What kind of birds do you usually find locked up?
Quimby: I have no clue.
Quentin: Jail-birds.

Other Books by Bob Phillips

All-Time Awesome Collection
of Good Clean Jokes for Kids

The Awesome Book
of Bible Trivia

The Awesome Book
of Heavenly Humor

Awesome Good Clean
Jokes for Kids

Awesome Knock-Knock
Jokes for Kids

The Best of the Good
Clean Jokes

Dude, Got Another Joke?

Extremely Good Clean
Jokes for Kids

Fabulous and Funny
Clean Jokes for Kids

Good Clean Jokes to Drive
Your Parents Crazy

Good Clean Knock-Knock
Jokes for Kids

How Can I Be Sure?

How to Deal with
Annoying People

Jolly Jokes for Older Folks

Laughter from
the Pearly Gates

Over the Hill & On a Roll

Over the Next Hill
& Still Rolling

Over the Top Clean
Jokes for Kids

Overcoming Anxiety
and Depression

Super Incredible Knock-Knock
Jokes for Kids

The World's Greatest
Collection of Clean Jokes

The World's Greatest
Knock-Knock Jokes for Kids

For more information, send a self-addressed
stamped envelope to:

Family Services
P.O. Box 9363
Fresno, California 93702